GET FRESH BOOKS

and profound. They speak to a restlessness that cannot be quenched—or drowned—by the promises of America. As an immigrant mother on her deathbed remarks, "I thought there'd be more."

—Olga Livshin, author/translator of *A Life Replaced: Poems with Translations from Anna Akhmatova and Vladimir Gandelsman*

PASSAIC illustrates affection for tenacious immigrant roots like no other with these heartfelt poems that greet us like "a rain of reminiscence and receipts,/ postcards sent from/ the other shore." After reading this collection, I'm convinced the Passaic River has a water spirit and a poet laureate, and that's paulA neves.

—Rigoberto González, author of *To the Boy Who Was Night*

neves' poems transcend the generic and move the Luso-American narrative into different spaces, not asking permission for her poems to think and bleed. They create a universe both doubling as reality and dreamscape. A place of created mythos that is ultimately country and home.

—Dimitri Reyes, author of *Papi Pichón* and *Shadow Work for Poets*

PASSAIC

poems

paulA neves

Get Fresh Publishing, A Non–Profit Corp.
PO Box 901
Union, NJ 07083

www.gfbpublishing.org

ISBN: 9798218522544

Library of Congress Control Number: 2024947573

Cover photos: courtesy of paulA neves

Author photo: Rachel Fawn Alban

Cover design, and typesetting:
culture glut llc / cultureglut.com

This book was typeset in Config Variable and Bembo Std.

In recognition of the Lenni Lenape peoples
whose ancestral homeland inspired so many
of the poems in this collection.

Povo que lavas no rio (Folk who wash in the river)
Que talhas com o teu machado (Who carve with your axes)
As tábuas do meu caixão (The boards of my coffin)
Pode haver quem te defenda
(There may be some who'll defend you)
Quem compre o teu chão sagrado (Who'll buy your sacred ground)
Mas a tua vida não (But your life, never)

—Amália Rodrigues

Still I dreamt the River Snowdrift. To my kin, I made no sense.

—Yona Harvey

My river waits reply.
Oh sea, look graciously!

—Emily Dickinson

CONTENTS

Passaic

from pahsayèk, meaning "valley" or "place where the land splits"

—The Lenape Talking Dictionary and Wikipedia

*We've heard all kinds of stories from the older generations that
when they were younger, they'd get to go and swim in the river.
And we've never during our lifetime ever seen that.*

—Sergio Rodrigues, NJTV News, 2017

On Monday, they may remember
Sunday morning with concentric rings,

Ironbound antiphons in the breeze,
fishhooks and faces abstracted on the green.

You should've been in church, but even then,
you pulled yourself out, to watch others

haul bluefish and bass, show them,
glistening and struggling, to strangers and kin,

declaring, "Here!" as if there was
no other proof of being.

And you—you made more of a line
than anyone, treaded mud to untangle roots,

mourned ducks whose bills dangled hooks;
wounds blurred colors of countries you'd left,

iridescent in the workday runoff,
and they all said and did nothing

in papers filed out of state.

By Sunday evening,
there is little unraveling:

Communion's long past
bait in hand, turn of head, Amen.

Ribs turn back to gill in protest,
livers sing the size of fists,

crows grow quiet on the rooftops,
geese huddle on loading docks,

trees clothe themselves in dusk.
A student asks, "What's Agent Orange?"

Monday morning late one century,
they may remember

how names were written on these currents.

No. They'll say they invented it,
subdivide and sell the waterfront.

And words will write themselves again
without us:

Oceans rising,
pray the puddles.

Oceans rising,
pray the lakes.

Ocean's rising,
pray Passaic.

Half-Hour Lunch, Renco Toy Factory, 1969

Daybreaks you forgive your firstborn,
your faces close enough to rhyme,

carry her to Senhora Francisca's door,
catch the carrinha to Jackson Street Bridge

over the dead river. The night school primer
tells you how to say "good morning"

to Baby Sister Grow-a-Tooth and Tumbling Tom
(you wonder if she makes him take his top off

so she can put it on).

The days are dolls and soldiers.
The days are arms and legs.

(The smell of sleep must haunt them too—
new moon in glass eyes.)

Noontimes you debate with other women
whether hen or cock made the best canja

you ate in your mothers' kitchens.
The wall-high window fans spin water

till river becomes air.
Senhora Francisca will tell you later,

"I'm sorry, I can't watch your daughter.
She screamed all day and vomited again."

At night you have no music;
you throw the lunch bones to the strays.

The light behind each window shade
is yellow like a prayer.

This Isn't Angola or Mozambique (O Preto)

after Carrie Mae Weems's
I Looked and Looked to See What So Terrified You

I looked and looked to see what would work.
I laughed in the vanity, eyes lined with kohl.

Caveira I was, with night years for eyes, you at 2
could not tell mother from skull on the cover of the *Times*—

Lord, at 19, with you, I felt as old as that Lucy
delivered by the mailman who, luckily, was Black,

perfect timing because you wouldn't eat your soup.
O Preto will get you! O Preto!" "No, I eat, I eat!"—

as I collected the mail for the Americans upstairs.
You never saw him on the stoop, but thank God you *knew*

just from his being that you'd better believe.
My bruxa eyes made you clean only half of your bowl.

Try me again. No child of mine will make others accuse
me of neglect. *This isn't Angola or Mozambique.*

Nap (Rocky Mtns—Come Again!)

*

you're still deciding what to dream
when the last rag-and-bone man
hawks his wares down Ferry Street

*

outside the oiled window shades,
sparrows, catbirds, whatever

calls you from the sycamores
(that twist like your grandparents' hands),

throws shadows like exclamations
across the crocheted bedspread.

*

somehow your mother never sleeps
with dishes waiting in the sink.

her waking looks like, you guess,
the burning hills of Buçaco forest

that she talked about at Sunday dinner once—
how every summer some idiot tourist threw a match,

to end it.

*

your father ate stewed rabbit and didn't hear
the details she borrowed about the apocalypse

from cousins and visinhos after church.

★

you never sleep again yourself,
whole nights waiting for him to come home,

burning just to catch a glimpse
of bird-shaped water pistols

or key fobs declaring, "Rocky Mtns—Come Again!"—
whatever presents he'd stolen from Port Elizabeth and Newark

lying on the kitchen table at dawn.

America Un-Admitted

that this one's face is half new moon full
mother's milk and father's coal tar
Chinese opera and Mardi Gras

gilded dust on dead sister's dresser
ace of clubs dogged
in brother's drowned rucksack

an overpass where the blood burned
into the earth who forgives … again
big sky sun where white is not

possum wisdom the neighbor shot
with amphetamine glint
in the noon dark sun

that this one's face is not
smoke and mirror just crème cacao
blood black angel in the snow

Warsaw ghetto where grandfathered stars
were only half seen in the half light
so the stars might have forgot

that this is Newark and Standing Rock
where Jesus look-alikes at JFK
learn customs out of 1938

and this one's face has seen Ra
this one's face has been crow
this one's face

and this one's face
is this one's face
you know

Three-Season Year

In the summer he made barbeques,
the noxious billow of lighter fluid

meeting match flames
over splintered sidewalk branches,

turning Nixon's plans and Green Stamp ads,
like everything, to ash.

He never bothered me with small talk,
never said, *You too can grow up to be president.*

He drank Pabst and muttered,
Bullshit.

In the autumn, he disappeared
down the storm cellar hatch,

bearing armfuls of arbor grapes—
Persephone's orphaned brother,

emerging again at Indian summer
with gallons of Canaan wine.

In the winter, he made barbeques,
the acrid smoke from dripping chicken fat

warm and comforting—
enough to save on gas.

Though he never admitted he was too cold
in wifebeater and work pants,

he never said, *Take this in to her.*
          She never said, *Take this out to him.*

The following spring
I hear he planted a kitchen garden.

Graciete

she taught me to play
potato skins

like a strop,
the peels eyelid thin—

because why should flesh
suffer

when meat matters most

in a linoleum kitchen
in a newark dim

pulaski street building?
the corner church

is st. casimir's problem
not hers,

so why should she light
a candle for fatima

be her own burden

when water beats
in the sink

sluices the chicken's cold skin
with abandon?

I will listen to her
just once more

while she cradles the blade
in one hand

insisting that I
unravel.

Independence Park

These aren't the days of wine and stories
or half-eaten merendas under the sycamores,

watching the kids hang from monkey bars,
the old Italianos roll bocce balls.

His game was malhas on Sunday afternoons
with the other rapazes at the old horseshoe pits,

to see who had the mettle to strike
the iron rod with well-aimed disks,

those tokens he'd afterward drop
with the stray cents and odd rusted screws

they both kept for no apparent use
in a Hellman's jar behind the door.

(I now keep this tradition myself
to hold down the corners of my house.)

After Mass she cleaned and complained to herself,
loud enough that the Polacos in St. Casimir's could hear,

about that marido of hers, out with the boys,
old men in their 50s or more,

making $3.75 an hour by then—
nothing compared to Independence Park.

Weekdays he saved die cuts from discarded lots,
threw them into a pail to sort through at lunch,

polished and pocketed them and went whistling home,
eager for Sunday, his boys and the sun.

On days he was late, especially if it rained,
she prayed that lightning hadn't struck,

that the machines hadn't crushed his hand or his foot,
like his cousin Ramiro, gone on disability

(though sometimes she wondered
what would happen if he did).

Like Senhor Serafim, also collecting,
and happy again in his life no doubt,

sitting in a clearing of pine and eucalyptus,
drinking the first of the baga

with good cheese and sausage.
But these aren't the days of wine and gossip.

Lately, he cuts through the park and imagines the glint
off the disk as it flies to marry the target,

a spark that makes the Fourth of July look
like the itinerant pop of illegal fireworks,

instead of the prescience already on their faces
years before the last fábrica closed.

She cuts up the chuck after piecework at Ford.
He comes home all wet, hangs his hat near the door,

checks his quarters for Social Security on a calendar there.
They both sit with me for the six o'clock meal.

She doesn't ask him how his day was.
Their silence speaks about "when," and "life is as it is"—

to start over tomorrow, work and look forward
to chartered vacations too soon over.

Dawn

Dawn, your fingers bright with tats of roses and bling,
don't throw a fit because your Portuguese Orion
strolls the park on break a couple times a week.
He's not hunting for some sweet young thing,
he says, just likes watching the people, pickup ball,
gets the feels, the peace he doesn't from working
in a body shop, remembering the blasted beasts—
stacks of trailers when this "beautiful, clean park …
was just a dump…" now "it's a whole new city"—
shinier than Troy (the smart-ass poet interjects)—"Huh?
I'm from the Ironbound," says Orion, whose real
name he asks to keep off book, but whose first initial
rhymes with "are," as in we are walking in the sun,
listening to our muses on our twists and turns.

School's Out: Newark, 1975

The lungs are a temporary house.
And, I am housed in a breathless city.

—Roger Reeves

memory is three-story, aluminum-sided
      where jagged lightning flies
            on humid summer afternoons

you sent us out on bikes
      you sew at secondhand machines
            needle strikes the cloth

lines lay out our life
      handlebars stream hours
            a house above our hands

rooms below our lungs
      you practice english on the bus

                we pop wheelies off the roof

11th Birthday

They are all here.
Neighbors, cousins, mother's coworkers,
primped in polyester on the plastic-covered couch,
their children with their hands on everything
(*mal educatos* as Ma would say—
except on special occasions).

To impress them, on my 11th birthday
I sit at the piano, the one Ma bought,
after two months of Saturday shifts,
from Maria Marques, because her daughter, Diana,
after just one year of learning herself,
started giving lessons and outgrew it.

"Va la." Go on, play us something understandable,
they urge, instead of all this jangling.
Then tell your sticky-handed brats to leave, I think,
when Diana, already a lady at 12, takes her place
beside me on the bench, turns to the last page,
and starts the count, quieting them instantly.

Surprise! I clank though my own "Happy Birthday."
Diana hums to keep the beat—futilely,
as everyone sings it in their keys.

How long this lasts I'll never remember.
Meanwhile,

the food waits on the table we never use:
Wonder Bread, ShopRite cola,
yellow butter crème cake from Coutinho's
decorated in cursive thin as veins
(from which those little fingersmiths
have already swiped the *day*).

Apart from this there are the staples:
potatoes, rice, the deep-fried cod fritters
they all call *balls,* which, if I look
at Diana now, would make me titter—
understanding, as I am,
how concerned they all are with *appearances.*

So, instead, I hit a wrong F-sharp on purpose
and offer it to Diana (whose conducting never wavers)
as small revenge for playing along with our mothers,
who wouldn't want us to misrepresent
why at other people's houses we get the stare of death
if we dare to entertain a "yes"
when we are offered
anything.

Jackie & the Latchkeys

★

Summer 1982. Patio under aluminum shade,
8x10 concrete over red Jersey clay.

Jackie Gonzalez sings Peaches & Herb,
"Reunited and it feels so *good* ..."

Jackie, the only girl on the block (I don't count),
calls her Florida boyfriends collect while we sit—

two-inch orange nails click cordless phone numbers.
I'm there for Mike, her little brother,

my b-ball & football co-conspirator.
Jackie & I throw down with the Sugar Hill Gang,

then dare the air, "Do you? Do you?"
when Rod Stewart sings,

"If ya want my body ..."
hers which I would, totally,

if not for her wedding at all of 16—
hell, her parents did it in *Habana* she claims—

but her parents are never around when she sings.

Her parents are never around when she sings
me—in my dreams—& neither are mine,

still working off their *Habana & Lisboa* goodbyes.
Yes, I want your body, working my nerve.

The boom box teases, but I'm all reserve.
"What are you saving it for, marriage?" Mike asks.

No (passing him the ball), for love, hopefully
(even at 13, a deluded romantic). Just then, Jackie blasts

"Don't You Want Me, Baby?"—& laughs,
like she knows something this good won't last.

This is the summer of '82—'81?
We practice all day out of the sun

to perfect our routines in the time that we have.
Don't you want me, oh-ohhhh-ooo-oh!

Space (or 1970s TV)

In order for us to have a future that's exciting and inspiring,
it has to be one where we're a space-bearing civilization.

—Elon Musk

We

were the

rockets of rooms

the *tripas* the heart the fire
watching black & white antenna
TV Battlestar Galactica. Imagine:
1999 was gonna be a rogue moon
we'd already lived through & going
back to the land (*ó terra!*) nothing like

how

the Marias & Josés (Joe-Zehz not
Hoe-Zayz) remembered when they
couldn't even handle the escudo to
to euro con(version) never mind
the dollar the dollar the almighty
$$$ pinned to Our Lady of Fatima
& José—for insurance—for—
Uncle Sam & Ma Bell & José I mean Joe

family head/factory hand always
changed the channel or turned it
off to save us while Mama Mary/
Maria explained that green cards
cost green—not like the kale-
for-soup-or-pasture-for-cattle kind
of saudades but for the payment
to the clinica overcharge for the

con(venience) of keeping the heater
at 50° all winter & the medico wants

more tests (still does). So little bro
& me laughed our *guts* out to keep
warm then adjusted our parkas &
mitts to imitate Apollo & Starbuck.
Only the Marias tell us no way it
was like that & our own Ma Maria
said we I mean I um "exagero'd"
if not outright lied. But I say space
is space & had to be reached

from there
somehow.

Transliteration (The Beautiful Game)

Alone, the family house
Blinds drawn on crooked basalt
Crooked as country boy's teeth
Daring to cut the light
Enough till it's clear as aguardente
Father drank before he found God
Gardener, who left the pitch to
His son, the footballer

I was, a girl hat-tricking two decades too soon.
Just one more minute, Ma—
Kicking the ball in the street till the sun
Lifted the fire over water again.
Madeira, you're not so far from
New Jersey.

Saving the World, One Scrimmage at a Time

Ntwadumela, he who greets with fire in Sesotho,
hails from post-World-Cup South Africa
by way of a grandfather and father's West Virginia,
attended Rutgers playing what America calls football,
a scholarship to study econ and pre-med bio,
then graduated to found a nearby tech startup—
says, "what I've learned … I'll always use it"—
does not worry how long he'll live in Canarsie, Brooklyn,
before moving on, smiles while scoring goals on a Newark
riverfront summer afternoon, a pickup with a Spanish-
speaking friend who says he's gotta run
when I start asking too many questions, who
Ntwadumela later confides is homeless, adds,
"If you go to Market Street, you still see a lot of them."
On a polished turf pitch in the middle of a renaissance,
he who greets with the energy of the sun declares,
"I'm not a politician. We are all people. I do what I can."

Lathe Operator

LightMaker.

"Lighting technician," you correct me
silently from the employee ID card,

the photo taken long before
pandemic,

when you sat at lathes
and shaped quartz bulbs

that pulsed outside
casino walls,

lullabies in arc lamps
you learned to fashion soup to nuts.

They light up Cristiano's torso
and a Rolex watch

in Times Square or above Route 22.

You—and we—had gifts—no matter.
You keep shaping, drilling, goner.

You keep shaping, drilling, believer.
Knurl the metal at its base—

these diamond shapes
hold promise.

Work

Ordered, making change at Burger King,
I didn't cop to knowing "who"
when high school classmates, taunting, ordered fries
again and again and asked,

"Who's that old bat in the window?
She know you?"

How could she know me, and
how could I know
how much plate glass her palm-framed face
had already looked through?

"Not all work is work," she always said,
"Take it from me"—

who traveled 3,000 miles
and one rush hour Broad Street intersection
to verify the gravitas of mopping, wiping, or simply waiting
had not been lost on me.

Later at home, she said, "You pretended not to know me,
but I know you—better than you think."
But what I thought was,
God, I'll be a journeywoman, just like you—

always polishing surfaces,
hoping to find what's underneath.

Return (Oranges at the Festival
of the Village Saint)

It's a child's color   or it should be   tasting like early summer
before it fades to the broom-sweep coat of the dog days.

—Carlo Matos

Augusts of our origins,
we put on best shorts and smiles,

rented Mercedes or BMWs whose wheels
crushed olive and eucalyptus leaves down the paths

along which someone had inevitably
picked winter oranges left for pith.

We strung up tissue banners with the locals,
watched the paper flutter from three light poles

that took two prime ministers to raise,
and waited for the band

marching from the chapel
(alheira-making ancestors long forgotten),

to play a dirge we all recognized
as praise for knowing one's own place.

The parade always stopped
the retornados in their tracks:

"This is lively," said the mother,
"Who died?" asked the son,

"Hóstia!" shouted the Host of Hosts,

from a grand new terra-cotta casa.

"You sure that house is big enough?"
The neighbor viúva (who long ago

stopped being someone's daughter)
cracked while peeling pith

for orange garnishes
on roast suckling pigs' lips.

It's not like Jesus, Mary, and Joseph
ever drove a Plymouth.

Burning Buçaco (The Pilgrims' Souvenirs)

I went to visit my father in the foothills,
at the villa he bought
after 20 years overseas.

Finally, after all of it—
these spacious,
well-appointed rooms,
pristine kitchen,
gleaming walls,
time on his hands.

This is how one lives
in the museums of the imagination:
20 years overseas,
but time passes
and counts for everything;
20 years elsewhere,
counting change
that he now spends
like water.

But it's summer,
and the mountains are dry.

Someday, they will find a cure
for what ails us.

Until then,
he spends his days like a general,
pacing the terrace
that so generously embraces
the whole of that house.
What views in every direction!
Each longing dispatched!

What isn't possible
when there's time enough?

Perhaps they've already found a cure
for what ails us.

Down below, at the foot of the garden,
the pilgrims returning
from a new miracle
stop for lunch and a rest.

They don't even know
what they have.

It just takes one ember,
one reckless thought,
one open passion
to blaze the museums
of this perfection.

Smother it and go!
Or else we won't have time
to redeem our indulgences.

Meanwhile, the old man,
after having paid
a third of his life
to live his dream,
spends the afternoon
pacing the terrace.

Sun without world.
Wind without breath.

You don't even see the flames
racing toward you.

The Simple Life

after Bruegel the Elder's The Harvesters

Jonghelinck might have had you believe
over candlelit dinner at his country compound—
pheasant with Portuguese pepper perhaps, sugared plums—

that the harvesters coming home from the fields
loved the evening road's dust,
their houses' plain girth,

because August reminded them
what they were made of, and left,

as if merchants were struck from different cloth,
as if there were no more marranos in Antwerp,
dreaming of New Amsterdam dark.

At the hearth, calloused hands pause
over bread and stewed rabbit on Sabbaths,
and we suspend our disbeliefs.

We walk warmly at dawn to the fields because roads,
despite their Roman-ness,
are what carry us:

We give ourselves over
to whatever's next.

And the fields, half gathered,
remember history better than most.
And the fallen roofs know, when winter rains,

which walls the wild currants
will overtake in the spring.

My Father's Last Sunday

for Luis
after Rimbaud and Modigliani

★

He turned Sunday to Monday
like water to wine,

stories he learned through
escola primária and

a 9th birthday spent spreading
sulfato on the fields,

so his father's corn, wheat, and rye
could rib his mother's broa,

the hard future
neither cake nor surprise.

He decided then
to leave the terra

behind for his father
and the flat-footed

to pound with their aguardente
at the peasant festas.

He decided to trade
Salazar for salt water,

float lighter than cork
on the waves.

★

He turned the calendar
by habit to Monday,

drove his Toyota RAV4
with canja in his belly,

his mother's recipe,
a light supper for Sunday.

The late afternoon drive
painted New Jersey's July

a Modigliani landscape,
art he'd never learn

in the window above
the teamsters' time clock.

Oh carotid promise,
you stick your neck out enough

working double overtime,
unloading the world's conscience

in Port Elizabeth-Newark—
25 years prioritize,

make stewards from stevedores,
no time to consider

whether Monday is midnight, slip
deck shines from sea-slick or steel,

crane operator gives
a thumbs up or down,

lift chain cracks
a thorax into crumbs

that feed the seagulls
your father's pomace,

your mother's bread,
your children's paid-for teeth

drifting.

The Latest Frida Exhibit
(A Prayer for the Fractured)

*I have no choice but to put up with them since
they are the ones who buy paintings.*

—Frida Kahlo

Frida, it's not tribute, fashion, or socialism
that knits my brows

while I consider your retablos and sewing kits,
take a selfie while

the halves of this American experiment
cannot meet—dresses and bodices

to defend—for or against?—this land
you weren't much impressed by,

save for San Francisco and New York—
Left and East—the rest they cannot

meet nor comprehend—but I digress.
My brow's furrowed for pondering (selfies or)

how to mend a wall, the broken backs
behind it, bones left in deserts so long

the sun's whitened them enough
to almost pass,

wall whose cracks even Diego's
powers could not camouflage.

But I digress, again. Do we always turn
to you to see with our Ray-Bans on

through your third eye—ah those eagles!—
because you know the answer,

though you cannot say? Or do we just
keep thinking that you do, keep paying

tribute—i.e., co-opting. Facts:
this land was always yours,

was made because canvas and pain
are wider and deeper than frontier.

You answer: America,
paint your own damned portraits.

Offerings, Ofensas

after an ad in the Lisbon Metro recalling the victims of the
International and State Defense Police (PIDE)

for more than a braid of a daughter's hair
or a son's milk teeth wrapped in chita
the priest-professor told you to believe

so you believed
in economies of ofertas
you believed in Fátima and fadistas

who sang of sailors and their strong sea
legs taking them anywhere but Tarrafal
far from your honeyed wax heart

far from the woman like your mother
who carried your perfeito coração

hoping the gulls would eat from her hand

hoping just one would have come
instead of PIDE to ask
what she had to offer

if she believed in her own ofensas—
perdoai as nossas...ai Senhor—
if she believed her feet were anchors

or there but for the grace of God
pillars of a house
where they'd set old smoke on fire

again and again insisting
with eyes the brass of chalices
that she shouldn't have

Personal Effects

And now for years I'll see your face
on well-dressed men older than you,

on buses running too late for the shift,
in restaurants where other diners gave you the check,

in union clinics where bones are set like borders,
in stalls where weekend hustling demands dollars.

Even unborn I shadowed you, whispered
as you crossed the corner to the bar,

"This is not where our intentions get filled!"
You cuffed me on the mouth once

for being, like you, a smart-ass little bit,
dragged yourself from wherever the buck had stopped

insisting time was "too much money to just piss."
You died in your own currency to prove it.

Sprit

Some feared to set the sprit; but I insisted …
I could sail as long as I could see.

—Jack London

And

now for years I'll see your face
on well-dressed men older than you,

electric buses running too late for the shift,
vegan restaurants where diners gave you the check,

      … union clinics where bones are set like borders,
… summer stalls where weekend hustling demands dollars.

You'd dragged yourself from wherever the buck had stopped
                     (I … knew this),
      insisting time "was too much money to just piss."

      I knew all this before—even unborn shadowed you,
whispered (in English) as you crossed the corner to the bar:

"This is not where our intentions get filled!" You laughed,

then cuffed me on the mouth once born—
dragged yourself from wherever—and who was

I for daring to be, like you, a sprit,
rising above everyone else in port?

There

are no epics about where the buck has stopped.
You ... died in your own currency to prove it.

I will not.

Capricornucopia (The Dream of the Goats)

Goats appeared at the door,
asking to eat the house from inside out.
It was Christmas, so we let them enter.
The drink-laden guests parted.

Sure-footed on the walnut-inlaid parquet,
the beasts made for the manger first,
ate the fake hay with unbridled relish.

The billy goat then eyed the end tables
my girlfriends and I had saved from curbs,
and that I had carried on my back
to whatever places we were calling home.

All the females followed billy boy's suit—
whatever they're called, girly goats?
I know what they are, but regardless,

everyone looked at me as if the goats
could see through walls—
an insight out of Freud or Foucault.
My new girlfriend looked pissed.

The goats made for the sofa.
"Who are they to you?" my girlfriend insisted.
Stuffing fell about us like snow.

The billy goat toppled the tree.
Blown glass ornaments blew everywhere.
Some shattered. Some dangled
from his horns like disco earrings.

"Androgyny went out in the '80s,
when you were still young,"
I heard at my ear.

I hoped it was the voice of the devil
I didn't know—a future lover perhaps,
her flutes as piercing, her heart as cloven
as any Pan I could ask for (and have).

But it was only my mother,
who whispered, "Did you ever turn on the oven?"
Then added, "You're starting to get whiskers, just like them."
Tender, the words went through me like a horn.

Mercifully, someone shouted, "They're headed for the table!"
And so the goats were. Like midnight buffet tourists,
they charged the sweetmeats, the Mouton Cadet,
the chanfana like grandma used to make.

"Cannibalism. At Christmas, no less,"
a faceless relative
tsk-tsked.

Let them.
Let them be goats.
Let them eat everything—

                              even the bones.

Casino Figueira da Foz

It doesn't translate. Figueira da Foz:
Fig tree at the mouth of the river, she'd tell coworkers,
whether fellow Portuguese or mildly disinterested Americans.

"Doesn't it mean estuary of the fig tree?" I contested—
that brackish place where a half-strung kid with a guitar
sang fados about a lightmaker—"Lighting technician,"

she corrects me silently from the employee ID card
next to the passport, Q-tips and other heirlooms in the drawer,
the photo taken the year or two before our trip,

when she still sat at lathes and shaped quartz bulbs
like those that pulsed outside the casino's walls.
"Impressive," she said—as any ramparts on our sightseers route.

Street pilgrims painted faces, traded fortunes, juggled fires,
painted portraits for cêntimos on the dollar.
A young man who braided plaits looked a little out of it

among the Vandals, Suevi, Visigoths.
He knitted a tired little girl's locks
with a patience and practiced art

she had no time for when I was the daughter
of the fishermen who mended nets
on postcards of the beach in the afternoons.

I did not mention this while she played roulette.

Gamblers

They met at the airport,
cleaning lounges for the VIPs.

His wife had left him in the early '70s.
She wished her husband had given her that courtesy.

Between them kids and grandkids rooted in the suburbs
(that her daughter's NYC girlfriends call a desert).

They drank red wine from thermoses
over weeks of lingering 30-minute lunches

that led from Friday nights at the Sport Clube
to nearly every Saturday on the boardwalk.

This went on for years.

But after anniversaries of hints and maybes,
all those comps she spent on him for rooms

and all-you-can-eat buffets,
she knew she'd never marry—not again.

So he started keeping his cards close,
and one night, without warning,

flew home, retired to his terra,
where turbine windmills

now cranked out electricity
for the shops that catered

to the tourists from the cruise ships.
Meanwhile,

her daughter tells her
with Jersey verve to forget about it.

Every Friday they have an early supper.
Then her daughter drops her off

at the bodega on the corner
and the Atlantic City bus.

Passing a Fibroid at an Off-Broadway Production of *Medea*

intermission at the ny theater workshop—
a bathroom line as long as gut,
but i was impatient and pushed through—
"hey lady, what the fuck?"

inside, my jeans barely down—
surprise! months after the procedure
that cut off blood to the *equivalent* of 12 weeks' growth,
i think of furtive teenagers in high school stalls.

but we're not like them, are we, medea?
we're tempered women—though I'm no queen.
still, you'd appreciate the irony,
when what is neither past nor promise slides out of you—

no medium for love or vengeance or remorse—
no ears, eyes, limbs, or perfect toes—
just a lump of undifferentiated muscle cells
from a hereditary broth.

"when you have children someday…"
our foremothers and the gods pronounced.
you were not meant to, observes the audience—
as if, for each of us, that were enough.

The Catholic and the Mormon
Who Met at Mardi Gras

I'm on a mission, chasing you, former chaser,
back to the Big Easy, where our masquerade began.
There, you showed me one Fat Tuesday was no baser
than the Monday to Sunday drag of those who pretend
protection with the gris-gris bits of home-to-work-to-bed,
scheduled sex, meals, workouts, movies in between.
Marriage. Some call that love, better than the head
space we got into on Ecstasy, when you confessed
you didn't need much (just a smile) to get undressed,
make many children for the afterlife with me.
As if! Ah, silly girl, parthenogenesis is Mary's deal,
and her son just a guy in a long dress, and
despite appearances, I'm not the boy of my father's eye—
just a girl who wants to find you again and proselytize.

The (Almost) Married Couple's Guide
to Tourist Traps

In Lamanai we learned how the Maya
might have sacrificed their hearts,

while we, lapsed vegetarians,
ate local spiced sweetmeats ourselves

to read the future in splayed
seagull carcasses along the Great Salt Lake

so that New Orleans Indians
would last until the next apocalypse

in that Baja town where men
are free as wives before the ceremony,

while we, women ourselves,
played possum for the Day of the Dead

so that, west of Oranjestad,
you could swim with fishes in the Mouth of Hell,

and I could watch you, with something
halfway between envy and regret,

until Oporto offered up a river of English wines—
so we could toast our never staying

long enough in one place.

Paralelos

While I stand with a coffee outside
the 7-Eleven in West Chester, Pennsylvania,

the day I introduced you to the eucalyptus, the looks,
the diesel carrinhas stirring up the dust,
is only a day.

While I stand outside the 7-Eleven,
good-morning Pennsylvanians
parade Americana, and we are having

our *sesta* (not siesta, that's Spain),
and wide awake, I am slinking
toward you, on hands and knees,

in my grandfather's widower's bed,
because we have the house to ourselves,
because he lies dying

in a convalescent casa in Pedreira, Anadia,
and I breathe the idea in your ear afterward,
as our bodies relax,

that we should rise the way he no longer can,
walk the kilometros of gravel and paralelos
in our flip-flops to visit him,

because you always wanted to go to Fatima,
and this is, as we stare at the rosary hung
heart-shaped above the headboard and laugh,

as close as we will get
to the cold fininhos afterward,
to the looks the regulars and barmaid gave us

when we tipped her too much,
two bedraggled Americanas,
each now standing outside

convenience stores somewhere.

Train to Lisbon

We took a train down the Portuguese coast and got drunk
on the wine and pastries packed in the trunk
we hoisted everywhere on our two-week Silver Coast junk-
et; bottles of tinto and pasteis eased post-argument funk.

Stopped sulking to ease wine and pastries from trunk,
after missing the express and waiting for hours in Cacém;
small bottles of *red* and *sweets* eased post-argument funk
better than bread bought fresh in Sintra the previous day.

We waited sullenly for hours in that park in Cacém.
"That's not how it happened!" I hear you object,
because we'd found Byron, not bread, in Sintra the previous day.
But lyrics aren't much concerned with the facts.

"That's not how it happened!" one always objects,
and sustenance is one of the fictions of our days.
Besides, lyrics aren't much concerned with the facts;
so this is what I mean put a different way:

Bread is just one of the fictions of that day,
like cumbersome love—I mean, trunk—and sweet drunken talk.
So this is what I mean put a different way:
When the train got to Lisbon, I walked.

Utah

Those we've forgotten have faces
of faded blues, drifting edges,
dun backgrounds, Indian feathers.

On the back of these postcards,
there are always a few well-scripted words:
Saltaire's carousel rings out its portents.
Random sparks in the kerosene air.

We wander the wreck of the lake, the pavilion, the flats.
Your people swam in the Great Salt Lake—I state the obvious.
Mine tried to pass at feast tables of roast suckling pig,
to become clean enough to earn Salazar's blessing.

It takes generations to invent a new West.
Seagull carcasses jewel every salted coast.

No Chelsea margarita can make us forget this.

Pearl River

after Ezra Pound and Li Po

When I wore my favorite jeans for you for the first time,
I stood in the street outside the Pearl River nervously waiting.
You emerged from gray coats and umbrellas of November rain,
all scarlet scarf and reclaimed thrift-store go-go boots.
And we went inside to shop for a life we were sure we'd have.
The store was thriving kitsch then. You bought me a tea ball
from a bin of many and mentioned how hot
the cheap red dresses would look on me:
"You're tiny enough to wear one," you said. Tiny.
A word I'd always hated until you.

At 37 I'd stopped scowling.
I wanted my tomboy tees and unmatched silverware
to mingle with yours forever and forever and forever.
Why should I buy anything more?

At 41 you said it's over.
You walked me down Broadway
as far as my World Trade Center stop
and kept going toward Brooklyn.
And you have been gone 15 months.
My Walmart boots make sorrowful noise when I walk.

You didn't look back when you went on.
The Pearl River is gone now. The window displays are all H&M,
the cheap dresses gone—lost to street vendors,
too many to choose from!
The leaves fall late this autumn, in wind and sleety rain.
Unpaired umbrellas still take up twice their space
on this narrow strip of Broadway.
They crowd me out.
        I'm almost 42.

After Hats

ask him about his hats
until he can begin to remember
not just stare at walls

after she's-not-his-first-rodeo leaves for work
after his requisite morning walk
after he rereads the scores

curses no one in particular
something like, "oh, go to the world!"
or vagabundo

what's the difference?
he does know to microwave his soup
he's familiar with plastic and scald

just ask him

Redaction

        _________________ distributed contaminants
that stir up the bottom sentiments (sic),
posing risks ___as well to ___ who consume
____ warnings and bans _____ are in effect.

Annapolis

That afternoon, the bosses drove us to downtown Annapolis,
promised lobster at that top-notch joint the locals all love.

Their assistant at the plant said it was "no expenses spared,"
how they "wheeled and dealed all the big cats." She winked.

But you are just a mere "technician,"
as you noted in the morning interview.

Why bother bringing me, your first and only daughter,
to your first and only interview in 30 years,

if you won't listen to what I tell you?
 "What I think my mother means,"

I glanced at you across the table
so that you'd get the hint,

"is that she has worked enough with quartz technology
to know the difference between all your bulbs."

I'll take 10 percent like an agent, I thought, amused,
instead of just the Amtrak ride.

At lunch, Bob and Carl, the brother-bosses who headed
The Specialized Lighting Corporation, strained for chitchat

over their cheesesteaks and crab bisque.
My mother, country girl at heart, didn't say much

over her chicken sandwich.
Neither did I, the vegetarian,

over a salad of arugula and pignoli nuts.

The Usual

after Hurricanes Irene and Sandy

And then there was a hurricane and then she was diagnosed and then she was dead … Empty midnight streets that read the sun deserted of beach resorts … A grad student wrestles with Derrida, but this is not a towel this is not a summer bedspread this is not a polyurethaned floor. This is not a roof tile held down with undersized nails. This is a hurricane and a year and another.

drought (the memory of trees)

a drought is upon us,
though the river will rise
& the grandfather elms
that limn the park paths
strewn with dog shit, while
signs nailed to their trunks
threaten $50 fines, drop
garlands of dried leaves
on the ground. it's more
halloween than an august
fraught with every summer
you no longer remember.
& the couple kissing
on a bench? they're not
together: they just met—
one is married, the other
committed to what was
once called an affair, booty
call, hook up. call it what-
ever, at least neither are
bots, seem actually into
the slick of their lips,
know where to look for
water in a drought. & what's
dead doesn't trouble a son
walking with mothers, one
who had him at 16, another
life, another drought before

they became. & leaves don't
bother the girl guiding tia & tio
up the city's shrinking steps
(parents deported, gone like
the green), the worn plastic
tips of their canes tapping
the ground like a metronome
marking the music of my name—
cuz don't think they aren't you
or me, or the homeless sleeping
in the shade of memory by
tennis courts where luxury
apartment club teams play like
nothing's at stake but the volleys,
missiles just missing the high-
schoolers flying their drones,
skateboards, scooters—bird flips
extra, but welcome as rain.

Caldeirada

Peel the potatoes, cut into chunks, and put in olive oiled water.

Chop in big rough pieces. 1 tomato.

Buy lulas at Seabra's. Ask them to clean them. Ask if they'll chop them up for caldeirada. If not, chop them youself— *tu nao es handicap!*

Chop the lulas in pieces, including the legs. No, don't chop the legs in pieces, just chop them off and use them. I remember Bob Burke's face when I stuff the legs in the lulas and took to work for lunch one time. Is not Hamburger Helper that's for sure!

Put in water with the pieces of potato and tomato.
I bought 2 lulas.

Turn stove on high to boil. Electric stove, not so good, but when you don't have a dog, hunt with a cat.

Use monkfish pieces.

Red snapper pieces.

Pollock pieces. Que? What do you mean like Jack-son Pollock? Pay attention. *Tas-me ouvir?*

No fish from Passaic. Even though one time you father brought some home …

Carrots. Scrape-peel. Chop e *põe na agua* to boil along with the lulas. That go in soon, not yet.

Potatoes and tomatoes.

Spanish or yellow onion. Because there's no Portuguese onion ah ha ha. Chop roughly (*what else is new?*) and put in with the other boiling stuff.
Ó my god. Is getting so hot in here. Is like climate change.

Bay leaf. Put it in.

Paprika. Sprinkle some in.

Oregano. Do the same.

Garlic or garlic salt. Whatever. What do you think?

Parsley. Of course it's fresh. From the quintal. Put it in. But not till the end.

Green pepper. Chop it and throw it. *Wha—?? Did I say against the wall?* How old are you anyway? You getting on my nerves, kid!

Turmeric or saffron for color. Just a pouquito. It's expensive you know. I don't care if Emeril says they're not the same thing. He's only half Portuguese.

Wash the salt off the fish chunks and throw in the ones that are, you know, "harder" first. Look, the fish are all in the water again! Only they're dead this time.

Cover pot and let it all boil. Don't aggravate me. It's done when it's done.

When it's almost done, pull apart watercress and throw it in. Until it's done.

Ó and a little white wine. I know you like to boozy. You don't get that from my side!

Remember:

Use flouring potatoes.

Use summer tomatoes. Or tomato paste.

You can use other greens, not just watercress.

Of course you salt the water. But if you don't wash the salt off the fish and put in a lotta salt, it'll burn like acid, kid.

I don't like pepper but do what you want.

Now get out of my kitchen.

Botánica

You told me to drive to the botánica
after settling accounts at the bank,

because bruxas might have that tea or retablo,
Our Lady's or another lost book of the bible.

Sango, though not your god, had a mother,
and Fátima, by other names,

still requires prayer, mortification,
though you'd settle for any tap water

that could cook plain rice bearable—
not that you'd eat it;

it's nothing like, never would be,
your arroz amarelo.

"This isn't a pharmacy!"
I would have barked months before,

and now, quixotic, still liable to.
Why drive half a block to a meter

when time, as you say,
even now, is still money?

And you know I'll be saying that too
when the bank sends the beneficiary forms.

But today, June 23,
we still breathe,

still believe in alchemies,
a gênio that casts out the shadows.

The botánica's door
was closed.

"Fechada?" Your voice
said more than you wanted it to.

Not a front or a folly.
"By appointment only."

Even saviors are apparently
on the clock.

We turned. You pushed away my arm:
"I can walk half a block!" Then, later,

"I bought two houses,
all my cars new, paid your tuitions,

an analfabeta."
Illiterate alchemist

who believed in a shadow
I cannot cast out.

Ma Watched Birds from Her Hospital Blinds
(Bird Slants)

another day
wrens were respite or regret

unending fable
that skin sheds

grief molts
we all take the bait

that what is underfoot
beneath the spinal birch

small birds
will not make us f(l)inch

red heralds
stillborn in the throat

will reemerge
(sp)arrow taut

bone and sinew snapped
like an afterthought

hours pared
to their mitochondrial light

give birth (*dar a luz*)
is how we hedge our bets

how our mother tongue
forgets the word for *missed*

how we explain
away the window's filth

why doctors entertain
where Daedalus got the wax

forgetting the sun
broken on our backs

Lazarus Squirms

and life tells me to embrace what is perishable
rather than choosing the record of what was.

—Rachel Hadas

the hospital solstice   in april
delivered her   home

                        new and pain clean

through each generation   each
peeled   layer   of   mask and gauze

pinched from drawers
        bright   bloodless   rooms

where   layers have use
                where   walls   remember

that she   rested

through june's drawn–   blind
attachment   to may

july's   straggler magnolias
august's curled   sycamore   leaves

too early   too late   for all
hallow's eve.   she rested and rose

to try legs she called   washed up   eels
turned   back into salt

73

denied the current   of
sashay and faith

proper balance   on woman-   or ungain-ly
hips   cradle of no more

betrayals   from which   she rises
now   on others' time

their bird bones stronger
amphibian apologies   to flight

rescinded   but they   retract their wings—
dragons   not saints   they can   rise

on their own—   why don't they?!
their bodies too

will leave them   in   emergency
berths   where she

plays solitaire with lazarus
names the old years,   dogs   she put down

asks   where's   jesus   now
that his mother's stopped cooking?

reminisces about birth   —lazarus squirms,

turns on the TV

Tuesday

If it's Tuesday,
the chemo will fail,

and February snow hangs like deer bellies
on backyard evergreens.

The garden fits onto a 1970s postage stamp,
but the deer show like gazebo brides

and approach at your offer of Indian corn.
You survived smallpox in rural Portugal.

You saw America on National Geographic TV
in your village's café grocery.

You knew the canyons of the moon by sight—
oh that skeptical blue retiring light

that calls the ocean sky to day,
that wakes you once more from midnight starts,

that brings deer to the edge of rush-hour streets,
makes birds mistake Monday for the sky.

Kitchen Sailor

after Amália Rodrigues

Caravela coffee cup, last of a pair,
has foundered in the dish drainer since the air

around your kitchen seagulls sounded life.
It doesn't matter your ex-sailor played your wife:

weeks of boiling, frying & washing floors for you
as if his life depended on it. He knew enough to fill the air

with as much apology as he could muster before he left,
factory cancer after 20 years not his idea of a mistress.

He drank lemongrass chá & sat with you before your final wreck,
had a plane to catch, said, "Be back soon. Desculpa for the mess."

He thought he meant his futebol scores & unmatched socks.
You hadn't been each other's for years by then, but breath

breaks hard against the past. He tells me now he soothed you with,
"You'll be better soon," is still in shock—

took the pieces of the cup he washed & broke in the sink
that afternoon with him to Lisbon as if it were a test,

a perfect artifact.

Math and English Word Problem
(3/4 sleeve blouse)

One eye sees night
as black as my irises
the other sees names
above mispronounced faces:

lips aslant
skin slack as defeat
hospital sheet grayed
by constant hands

3/4 sleeve blouse
worn for the factory office
dried stain on the cuff
our shared AB+

black running shoes
Atlantic teal accents
at the end of the stretcher
archipelagoes lost

at the end of the stretcher
the physician mouths "gone"
in 10 or 12 syllables
easy enough math

in 10 or 12 sentences
easy enough life
in 10 or 12 decades
we'll all be on Mars.

But could someone repeat
that the soles are unworn
before the variables come:
DNI— DNR—

acronyms meaning
I thought there'd be more.
My brother and I are
grayed like old times

our father undone
our mother
three decades on
the three of us are

the two of us again.
Ask the doctor are you sure?
Nod. Say "thank you."
Go on.

Amenities

*

The backyard peaches rotted on the tree this summer,
flayed by rain till July 4th fireworks

appeared for sale in the LA Fitness parking lot
beside the new luxury apartments with "curated amenities"—

swimming pool and onsite Starbucks.
Half your salary on a studio rent.

Oh right, the backyard peaches.
There were like 50 pounds worth

last year, most still ziplocked in the
freezer like bodies waiting to be ID'd.

*

The cat's been at the vet's since Thursday.
Now I think after 16 years she wasn't all that

friendly to begin with—feral creature in a saltbox.
But she has green eyes like patinated pennies

in the cornerstones of single detached dwellings,
and still will when I put her down, though now

it's all about the cryptocurrency.
At the corner deli,

I order my peppercorn turkey provolone wrap
because I'm not vegan, and it's just lunch,

30 minutes too short to save the planet
or my street, a quarter mile from one bridge

to our latest re-birthed city,
where cutouts in the construction paper sky

float to earth like blessings and lead flakes
to land on signposts that threaten panhandlers

with $500 fines.

★

In another town across the river,
hint: the latest one becoming Brooklyn,

I turn to you during a documentary about Afghanistan
in the independent movie house

and say, "That woman cooking naan is only in her [insert age]
but looks so much older than us."

We shake our heads in practiced disbelief,
confident in our unbuttered popcorn.

The woman, meanwhile,
surrounded by her daughters,

says, "I'm [the subtitles insert her age] and never learned to read …
… it's up to these girls now. Their father is too old to work.

They are now my sons."

*

NPR reports that migrants under the new policy
can no longer seek asylum

to escape violence they have no proof
was violent enough.

*

More new brick-faced "luxury apts." going up by ShopRite—
on the site of the aluminum bat factory

whose boiler blew in '80 and killed an electrician,
who may or may not have stopped

at the liquor outlet on his drives home
like my father used to before he got his green—

look a lot like the nursing home across the street
that my mother and the neighborhood committee

prevented from going condo in the '90s
(the traffic and parking were already bad enough),

but that fortunately had a ground floor room for her
to die in in the 2000-teens.

After factory cancer, hip and heart breaks,
it was nice to have convenience.

Uncited

> *... words—*
> *whether we like it or not—*
> *stand in a time of their own.*
>
> —Adrienne Rich

My mother has been absent 45 months. Has been.
The present perfect progressive tense describes
an action that began in the past, continues in the present,
and may continue into the future.

I find this definition, uncited, written in my daily
to-do list, along with other doggerel
I riffle through to find the page
where I can cross off "pay property tax."

She has been gone, as in, "I'm out!" three and ¾ years.
I pay the third-quarter property taxes she used to jot
on the bakery or insurance agency wall calendar—
free at Christmas because that's how

she kept American time, her themes cut out for her.
She will have been something for four years soon,
her molecules rearranged, her clothes beginning to tell,
hung day and night in every closet, as ripe as July

peaches on the roofline branches of the tree she planted,
careful cultivar of Pathmark pits watered with sweat
and fertilized with could or would have, "modals
of lost opportunities," which I cannot reach,

the way I could not pluck the Adam's apple of the man
who slowed his car at the corner of Monroe and Lafayette
to troll "hey mama!" along the outlines of her blouse and skirt.
What could my 7-year-old fists have done to him, regardless,

while holding her hand to cross the street?
Or to the man who tracked her in the maze
of Military Park's underground garage one afternoon,
that she mentioned offhand decades later like a latter-day

Ariadne unraveling the tacit threads of how to "survive,"
which might have helped me grasp the finer strands
of my manager's remarks at my first review that
"the man is always ready," and not just to

unquote my English.
That it sometimes helps if you smile.
But not a lot. Luckily, they will all have been
dead now longer than my count.

Will have. Molecules rearranged.
"The future perfect tense indicates that
an action will have been finished or perfected
at some point in the future."

Memoir

I unearth what
I thought I'd never see again:
crumbling grade reports from Ann Street School
in dusty manila sleeves,
inoculation proofs from a defunct clinic on Ferry Street.

I bear my generation's smallpox stamp,
intricate as an August moon,
on my upper left arm near the shoulder joint.
I have no offering more significant.

She, however, bothered to keep:

President's Council on Physical Fitness card.
Harrison Driving School certificate.
Arlington orthodontist's appointment reminder.
Livingston College acceptance letter.

More tarot than fado. But so what?
She had all the evidence and more to prove
she married, made a child, planted a tree.
But where's the book that all these pages don't quite make?

She hasn't written it yet, she admits,
though all of it proceeds from her,
a rain of reminiscence and receipts,
postcards sent from
the other shore.

Red River

When I forget a dead relative's name,
the village beauty sends it like a kitchen fan
gusts the scent of chicken hearts and
rice simmering on a hot June evening
too long ago. Oh. Did you think this was
going to be one of those meditations
on mortality and stoves? Nostalgia for
a stolen childhood bicycle? No. Because

when I am riding memory hard like
Montgomery Cliff going up against
the Duke in *Red River,* in an America
of scattered pots and stampedes, I hear
dead relatives' names. When I don't
remember that beauty is dead (my
father too, though he still never pays
what he owes), I feel guilty for asking,

guilty that the only thing that still fills
this vastness is those damned chicken
hearts browning in the scratched skillet,
small prices to pay for small lives, but
those big broad rodeo smiles would have
you believe so many things, cowboys
always ready to play their hand, and you.
What? That's not the thing to

say, right? You work hard all your life,
dreams and anything possible, and
I can't remember all the tumbleweeds.
Something about don't get into cars with
strangers, don't stand near the subway
tracks, don't wander at night into those
neighborhoods, don't say or act like you
mean it (right, Monty?), don't cross state

lines while pregnant, punctuate wars
(unless dinner is on the table), hide your
gun, show your gun (as long as there's
a gun), wear your skin or a scarf or your
name or *flash* you're asking for it, and
even if you're not, you'll drown quietly
and learn absolutely nothing unless it's, if
you're lucky, what your mother remembers.

A Portuguese on Retreat in Red America

We saw that the birds are really aggressive to songs by their next-door neighbors … but once there is enough distance between them, they don't understand the songs anymore … It's like if you speak Portuguese in Portugal, you can probably understand Spanish, and you might understand French, but if you keep going further and further away, eventually you'll hit … languages that are unfamiliar, that you can't parse.

—Kaiya Provost, the American Museum of Natural History, Smithsonian Magazine, Dec. 12, 2018

I sit writing at a field desk
from a war:

US Army—Korea or Vietnam—
worth more if it was Civil

the innkeeper, stepping out, says.
It's vintage from eBay

or handed down from someone
before her who cared

for such—
she can't remember.

I shrug. The spring-loaded
door behind her slams.

I jump as if it was
a gunshot, of course.

It's June, on a farm,
porch swing evening.

I sit at a desk from a war
fought on the front lawn

of every city
where I am from

when a cardinal
appears with a whistle and trill—

appears too red,
a loud red—

to compensate for
such a small crest?

No. That's not always
the way it works.

Or maybe a menstrual red
that soaks through

the quiet on the fence.
It's useless to write this:

Red of waiting for carnation days,
for the mother I wished for,

still write to on my posts,
the mother who pretended

my father died in Angola,
fighting against independence.

Oh, the romance.
And something else:

Blood she's had enough of—
too many white cells

fighting the rest,
consuming the flesh,

the incarnation—encarnação—
unholy alliance

of body and history.
Fine. Ok. Believe

that's not how it works.
But shamans and the dead say

when cardinal appears,
pay attention to circulation—

what comes around.

Dirty Martini & Boilermaker: A Love Story

I tell you my folx met in a bar
back in the days when August was hot

and it took all weekend to say goodnight,
while we keep so longing like it was swiped

from a late 20th century noir. Natch.
At least neither of us is proposing a toast

to facial recognition in the transom AC
or mistaking the ocean for some kind of brine:

polyethylene and water slip all over each other. So,
here's to someone conceding there's not enough light;

to the smoking asphalt reminiscent of bees
(oh, the last one that stings stays perfectly intact);

to pretending sunrise will usher our flight,
glass-rimmed penumbras as promising as Mars.

Living Dangerously

Yes, it's true.
I chase an aspirin or antibiotic
with a martini, or a few,
when it's open bar at a party
so as not to be rude
or appear ungrateful for the pleasure
of the three swollen olives
at the end.

I cannot lie.
I have picked up many noodles
slipped from the fork
onto the weeks' unwashed linoleum
before I could check if they were al dente enough
and bit them then or threw them back
or ate them standing
if they were perfect.

I acknowledge it.
I have tried on all the size 7 ½ shoes
and some others besides
on many reputable racks
and walked around barefoot in between
on soggy winter carpeting
because I liked even the hint of unbroken leather insoles
against my unwashed skin.

I have never been the type
to keep my hands away from nose or mouth
when walking crowded hallways in public
and never pushed the long bars of stairway exit doors
with my covered elbows
so that contact with others' particles
would be virtually
impossible.

When I'm feeling dangerous,
I microwave my lunch in reused
plastic wanton soup containers
or sometimes even in the Styrofoam
of the steamed-vegetable special
so that the thin, invisible film of released fumes,
along with the "negligible" microwaves,
will inoculate me a little at a time
from the inevitable.

Transcript

you remember her face like a postcard from the sea:
the faded blue, the drifting edges,
the dun background, stiff seagull feathers.

★

luminescence means
you could take for granted again
the taste of pennies on your own tongue.

★

unpaired umbrellas still take up twice their space
on this narrow strip of Broadway.
they crowd me out. i'm almost 42,

★

in the autumn
he disappeared down the storm-cellar hatch.
the smell of sleep has always haunted us—

★

the elevator opens into the apartment,
and the lines that vanish in all of us
are dormant seeds in window boxes:

★

the woman who was once your mother's age
when secret police asked what she had to offer

should not have stayed in–country
to set old smoke alight,

should not have insisted
with eyes of polished copper

★

how the Maya must have sacrificed their hearts;
a new moon on the bone of winter night.

★

he emerged with gallons of new wine.
though, like the wedding jugs at Cana,
they never seemed to run out.

★

childhood nights, the floor is ceiling,
and the overhead green-yellow bulb
out of a reproduction of the *Night Cafe*

is so bright it might blind,
if not that the throat closes so fast,
it automatically shuts the eyes.

★

reflection reveals we are only carbon deep,
no body to eclipse the space of what's left,
to fill the four corners of each year with a room.

★

i'll leave my longing and your house alone.
he planted a kitchen garden in the spring.

★

when you close your eyes, will you still see
through the crosshatch of shroud

the small beauty mark, wine-dark mole
in the center of the eyelid,

covering the sailor's eye
i inherited from you?

★

this shiny-eyed sadness is only a reminder.
outside, the summer ache of spiders spins the air.

★

over friendly drinks, she says,
timing is everything,

and I reply,
fractals,

the way some people say
bullshit

like it was
liminal

★

could you give me something to eat? he says,
i'm so hungry,
his windbreaker streaked by mid-November,
his cap a half-pulled cork,

and i am tempted to respond, *sir, we are all hungry,*
but of course I don't—
tuck my guilt under my arm,
my mouth caked dry for lunch.

holy water (the second coming of drought)

monday night. i've traveled to the house where i grew up. where my parents once lived apart, and still do. where my mother once lived alone, and still does. to check on her dogs that now are my cats. her tenants have been caring for them while she's been in portugal for a month. i hire a pet sitter instead. once if not twice a week, i check in on things. my therapist says that's a good thing. i let the dogs out. i play with the cats, who play dead cerberus. i put on my running shoes. i head for the park, where i played tennis with my brother during summer vacations. or strolled sunday mornings instead of being in church. this humble municipal acreage is my lot. this summer has been unrelentingly dry and hot. in this winter that is like dogs and cats. a drought is upon us, and we say so what? it's may and october, and the romance is dog shit and dried leaves. blue-eyed tony kisses dark-eyed maria on a nearby bench. only the irish have moved out to bergen county, and we're following suit. few of us remember what's what: tony and maria met in a factory. tony and maria actually just met. tony and maria are both portuguese. they started before my father left? someone hasn't told us yet. how to look for water in a drought. how to be divining rod and arc. i wonder as i sprint. why the twilight is perfect. i'm rounding the path at a clip. why is the twilight perfect? i finish, and the haze and heat that have built up all day grant me the serenity to notice what can't. and for all that, a single line of sweat rolls down my back, moisture too salty, too little, too late. to save the trees or myself. don't hold it against me or them.

There (Else)

The realtor calls and informs:
cousins have come to cart away all
the furniture they could.

"Que pena!"—what a shame (pity or waste),
she says they exclaimed. How long has it been
since they first brought knives,

forks, plates, carried the heavy mobílias,
crates with bravado, to fill what walls, ceilings,
and floors call a space, what my mother

just called "back there," superstitious as always
about shades of possession and possessed,
as if even then it was already "pena,"

the feather that blows out the windows
the realtor says won't pass the inspection
for the ex-pat tourists who'll buy it.

She tells me how much it will cost
for certificates, registrations, commissions,
how much the government will take,

and I think of everyone like me
who's flocked back there for romance.
"Ask your lawyer how much for the closing,"

the realtor adds, reminding me,
"A house just can't sit there empty, right?"
My mother answers for us. She stares

from a doorway of cinderblock, mud, memory,
18 years old, white kerchief and apron
damp from farm sweat and runoff,

bare feet and hands too big for pretty,
perfect for working and dying anywhere
else.

Kmart Pantsuits Picture Day

Velour sweater and polyester,
school-gym-basement-cafeteria;

the yearly lensman said *smile*—
pretend that sour milk and memory

aren't artifacts or money.
And for this you left the campo dirt,

let the factory break your back.
Did you misunderstand what Earth is?

Why else buy me Kmart pantsuits—
so that everyone in school would know

all the worlds you lost would not
appear with cartoon certainty

in every corner of our house?
Yet, for you, for this, I smiled

like every day was picture day,
and Kmart would never close.

Superfund

The Lenape had lived in the wooded hills for centuries … When the federal government created the National Priorities List …

—Michael Sol Warren and Andrew S. Lewis, "New Jersey's
Lenape Nation Fights Ford's Toxic Legacy"

Superfund. It sounds like a caped cartoon hero
your garotos watch on Saturday mornings before you
leave for your second job at Suzie's Coiffure, rinsing
the thinning pelts of senhoras of a certain idade you
can't imagine ever reaching, but 1980 is your year—
so proud your photo made the cover of the company's
annual report (still the village beauty, even the manager
says so), and the company is not even the Ford factory
your own mãe cleaned toilets in before she rose to
sewing vinyl bucket seats, praise Deus—those bathrooms
were dark and dank as iron mines in the woods by
the river in the newspaper the English teacher assigned.
Those poor lost Indians. What is it with Americans? And
why does your daughter say you're part of the problema?

Ida (Let the Water In)

★

The windows wail every time it storms.
I tell myself I'm gonna write that song.
But it all ends up in plastic—bottles or
bags torn from perfume samples some
mother got for all her miracles spent at
Macy's beauty counters, waiting for the
lottery or Atlantic City slots to purify her
like the waters at Curia—here, here's the
Rx, wait, it's all running together, I mean
the fix, to prove miracles do occur—from
the Latin for occurere, which sounds like
the Portuguese for "correr"—wait, it's
from the same damn family. I'm never
going to outrun this.

★

Rivers, cleanse me weekly with 500-year storms.
I always wanted a pool … in my living room. I say
it's all a poem. I say it will go viral. I say not in my
lifetime. But just in case I'm wrong, we may grow
gills again. Oh, omnipresent plastics and old PCBs!
Though bags and bottles rise, make mountains
out of … best laid plans, at least the economy's
renewable. Something will bail us out—*have faith
in technology,* say billionaire rocketeers. Float on

cryptocurrents, when the tide is out. Cuz none of
it will matter when the moon is full. None of it will
matter when there are no shores to home. I mean
Om. My eyes are getting tired. They keep seeing
the same things.

NOTES

"Half Hour Lunch, Renco Toy Factory, 1969"—*carrinha* is a bus, van, or sometimes, colloquially, a truck; *canja* is chicken soup or stew in Portuguese, Brazilian, and Cape Verdean cooking.

"This Isn't Angola or Mozambique (O Preto)"—*o preto* can colloquially mean a bogeyman or, literally, the black one; *caveira* is a skull; *bruxa* is witch.

"Nap (Rocky Mtns—Come Again!)"—*visinhos* are neighbors.

"Independence Park"—*merendas* are a snack; *malhas* is a game like bocce ball but played with stones or disks; *rapazes* are boys; *marido* means "husband"; *baga* is a red wine varietal; *fábrica* is a factory.

"Space (or 1970s TV)"—*tripas* means guts.

"Transliteration (The Beautiful Game)"—*aguardente* is a wine spirit and literally translates to "burning water."

"Return (Oranges at the Festival of the Village Saint)"—*alheira* are traditional non-pork sausages that fifteenth-century Jews made during the Inquisition; *retornados* means "the returned ones"; *hóstia* is the communion wafer at Christian services and has various other meanings; *viúva* means "widow"; "roast suckling pig" is also called "leitão" and traditionally served with orange slices.

"The Simple Life"—*marranos* is a pejorative term for Spanish and Portuguese "new Christians."

"My Father's Last Sunday"—*aguardente* is a wine spirit and literally translates to "burning water"; *festas* is a festival; and *canja* is a chicken soup or stew in Portuguese, Brazilian, and Cape Verdean cooking.

"Offerings Ofensas"—*ofertas* are offerings; *fadistas* are fado singers; *Tarrafal,* on Cape Verde, was a camp where the Salazar regime incarcerated social or political deviants; *perfeito coração* means "perfect heart"; *perdoai as nossas ... ai Senhor* means "forgive us our sins ... oh God."

"Capricornucopia (The Dream of the Goats)"—*chanfana* is a traditional Portuguese goat or mutton dish oven-stewed in wine.

"Gamblers"—*terra* means "land" or "home."

"Paralelos"—*carrinha* is a bus, van, or sometimes, colloquially, a truck.

"Botánica"—*bruxas* are witches; *arroz amarelo* is yellow rice; *gênio* means "nature," "temperament," or "genius"; *analfabeta* means "illiterate."

"Ma Watched Birds from Her Hospital Blinds (Bird Slants)"— *dar a luz* literally means "give to the light."

"Kitchen Sailor"—*chá* means "tea," and *desculpa* means "sorry."

"Superfund"—*garotos* are kids; *idade* means "age"; *mãe* means "mother"; *Deus* means "God."

"Ida"—*Ida* refers to the hurricane and also means "departure" in Portuguese and Spanish; *correr* is the verb for "to run."

ACKNOWLEDGEMENTS

Poems in this book have appeared, sometimes in different versions, in the following publications:

The Coop: A Poetry Cooperative: "holy water (the second coming of drought)" and "Personal Effects" (appeared as "Spirit")

Journal of New Jersey Poets: "Passaic," "My Father's Last Sunday," and "Amenities" (2020); "Botánica" (2019)

Newest Americans: PoemQuest: "Dawn" and "Saving the World, One Scrimmage at a Time"

Pilgrimage Magazine: "Kmart Pantsuits Picture Day" and "Nap (Rocky Mtns—Come Again!)"

Platform Review: "Drought" and "Uncited"

Quiddity International Literary Journal: "Burning Buçaco (The Pilgrim's Souvenirs)"

Red Fez (Issue 133): "Independence Park"

The Red Wheelbarrow: "There (Else)"

"Dirty Martini & Boilermaker" was featured in *Moving Words,*
a project by Arts By The People.

"Passaic" was the 2020 NJ Poets Prize Winner.

"Transliteration (The Beautiful Game)" appears in *Divine
Feminist: An Anthology of Poetry & Art by Womxn &
Non-Binary Folx,* curated by Marina Carreira (Get Fresh
Books, 2021).

"The Usual" won Honorable Mention in the 2016 Topanga
Messenger Contest.

*Special thanks to the City of Newark, the County College of Morris,
the Sundress Academy for the Arts, Portuguese Beyond Borders
Institute, and FLAD, whose support afforded precious time to develop
these poems.*

*A number of poems in this book are included in the chapbooks
capricornucopia (the dream of the goats) (Finishing Line Press) and
Shirts & Skins (Shine Portrait Studio Press).*

www.ingramcontent.com/pod-product-compliance
Lightning Source LLC
Chambersburg PA
CBHW041558160726
48006CB00042B/2146